AVI

All About the Author™

AVI

TAMRA ORR AND MICHAEL A. SOMMERS

ROSEN PUBLISHING®
New York

Published in 2016 by The Rosen Publishing Group, Inc.
29 East 21st Street, New York, NY 10010

First Edition

Library of Congress Cataloging-in-Publication Data

Orr, Tamra.
Avi / Tamra Orr and Michael A. Sommers. — First edition.
pages cm. — (All about the author)
Includes bibliographical references and index.
ISBN 978-1-4994-6276-0 (library bound)
1. Avi, 1937—Juvenile literature. 2. Authors, American—20th century—Biography—Juvenile literature. 3. Children's stories—Authorship—Juvenile literature. I. Sommers, Michael A., 1966- II. Title.
PS3551.V5Z768 2016
813'.54--dc23
[B]

2015024381

Manufactured in China

CONTENTS

INTRODUCTION

His paper landed on his desk with an ominous thud. Written in red was the teacher's discouraging comment, "Your work is very sloppy. Why don't you proofread?" Edward Irving Wortis, known to his family as Avi, hung his head. This was not the first time he had seen comments like this on his homework assignments. He did not mean to turn in messy papers, but writing just was not easy for him. Letters ended up in the wrong order. Words were difficult to spell correctly. His hard work ended up looking careless, instead of determined.

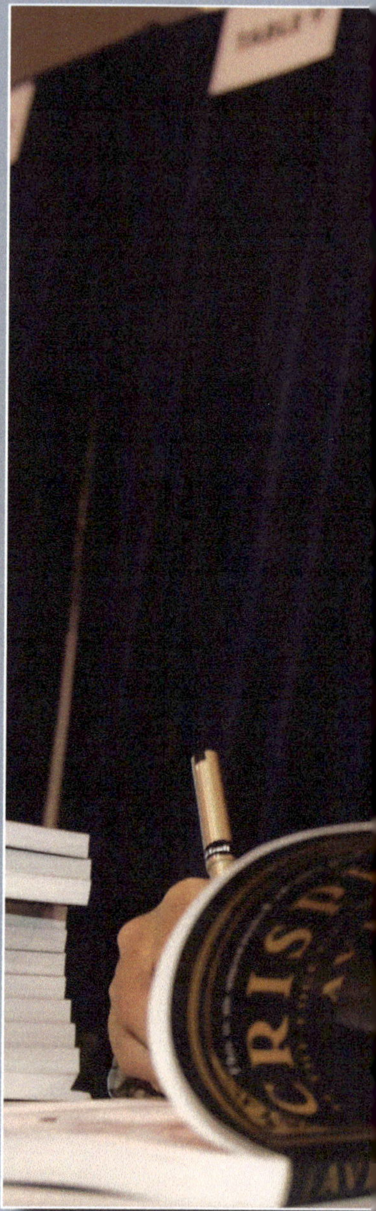

What Avi did not realize was that the main reason his papers were messy was because he had many of the symptoms of dyslexia, a condition that makes it harder to recognize and understand letters as well as words. As he told Reading Rockets in an interview, "It wasn't being sloppy. It was just this nature." In a live chat interview with the New

Even though his teachers did not encourage him to become a writer, Avi's passion for telling a good story won out.

York Public Library, he added, "I was always being told I was a bad writer, but in fact it was because of this other thing."

Avi's frustration did not end in high school. When he got to college, all those years of negative comments had built up, and he did not want to take any English classes. "I didn't take any of those requirements," he admitted in the interview. "But I was reading and writing voraciously. I sort of just didn't know any better, and kept going."

If Avi could have looked into the future, he would have been astonished to find out he would not only get better, but he would become an author known all over the world. He would win prestigious awards and captivate readers of all ages with stories ranging from edge-of-your-chair thrillers to historical fiction, animal tales from the Dimwood Forest to the award-winning modern classic *True Confessions of Charlotte Doyle.*

Despite his teachers making it clear they thought he would never become a writer, Avi started writing plays. At age thirty-three, he wrote his first book for young readers, *Things That Sometimes Happen: Thirty Very Short Stories for Very Young People* (1970). Five years later, he published his first novel, *No More Magic.* Since then he has written more than seventy novels for readers of all ages, including his Newbery Award–winning series about Crispin, a peasant boy living in fourteenth-century England. In 2015, Avi added *Catch You Later, Traitor* to his list of books. It focuses on a twelve-year-old dealing with Communism in the mid-twentieth century.

In 2005, Avi stated in an interview with the New York Public Library that when he writes his books, his primary goal is simple: to tell a good story. Fortunately, despite his teachers' criticism, he has done just that for thousands of readers and, hopefully, will continue to do so for years to come.

CHAPTER ONE

WRITING IN THE BLOOD

Perhaps it should not have been a huge surprise to Avi (pronounced AH-vee) that he ended up a writer—after all, the literary gene was certainly in his blood. Avi's family included many writers and storytellers. One of his great-grandfathers had been a professional storyteller and singer at Jewish weddings in Ukraine (a former republic of the Soviet Union). His job was to entertain wedding guests by telling stories, both sad and funny, about the bride and groom. Another great-grandfather wrote romance novels about poor Jewish girls who always fell in love with and then married rich gentlemen. Avi also had a grandmother who wrote plays and an aunt who was a journalist. His father, Joseph, was a psychiatrist, and his mother, Helen, was a social worker. Both of them published many works on subjects related to history and the sciences.

As Avi, his twin sister, Emily, and older brother, Henry, grew up, their house was often full of family members who dropped by to share stories. Helen read to the children every night. Surrounded by books, it was little surprise when one night, even before starting school, Avi announced to everyone he had taught himself to read. As he recalled in an interview, "When I was five years old—or so the family legend has it—I appeared at the dinner table screaming, 'I can read, I can read!' Alas, the legend makes no reference to what it was I read. True or not, that this story was told with pride and amusement suggests how important books were to me—and my family."

Once he learned how to read, Avi did not want to stop. He devoured adventure stories and mysteries, novels, and fairy tales. He read classic and modern literature, not only for children, but for adults as well. He also read and then traded comic books but could do so only from the front porch. Helen thought they were much too violent and would not allow them in her house.

Avi's childhood was spent on Hicks Street in the Brooklyn Heights neighborhood in New York, where he read just about anything he could get his hands on.

Although Avi and Emily were born in Manhattan, New York, on December 23, 1937, by the time they were a year old, the family had moved across the East River to Brooklyn. From almost the beginning of his life, no one called him Edward or Eddie. Emily could not say that name and instead called him Avi. The name stuck!

In Brooklyn, the Wortis family lived in an old four-story brownstone in the historic neighborhood of Brooklyn Heights. One floor was used for Joseph's office, which was where he saw his patients. Avi spent his entire childhood in this home on Hicks Street, until he went off to college.

When he was quite young, Avi especially enjoyed animal stories. His favorites included Thornton W. Burgess's tales about Peter Rabbit, Buster Bear, Jerry Muskrat, and Bobby Coon.

BEASTLY BOOK

Memories of his favorite animal tales inspired Avi when he began writing his own stories. In 1972, he wrote a story for young children called *Snail Tail: The Adventures of a Rather Small Snail*. Many years later, he added to this by writing *The End of the Beginning: Being the Adventures of a Small Snail (and an Even Smaller Ant)*.

His love of animal tales led Avi to write about the wonderful animals of Dimwood Forest. The first book in the series, *Poppy*, was published in 1995. In this book, the title character is a shy mouse that is forced to overcome her timidity and battle a mean old bully of an owl in defense of her home and her freedom. Poppy, along with her slang-talking mouse boyfriend, Ragweed, and a grumpy porcupine named Ereth proved so successful that Avi wrote four sequels: *Poppy and Rye* (1998), *Ragweed* (1999), *Ereth's Birthday* (2000), *Poppy's Return* (2006), and *Poppy and Ereth* (2011).

In 2001, Avi published another animal tale, *The Good Dog*. Set in Colorado, this adventure tale revolves around a pet malamute named McKinley who is torn between staying with her master, Jack, and joining a pack of wild wolves. Told from the dog's point of view, Avi hoped the book would satisfy the pet owners he knows who often wonder what their animals are thinking about.

Avi has also written two books about a raccoon named Amanda in *Keep Your Eye on Amanda* (1996) and *Amanda Joins the Circus* (1999).

In *The Good Dog*, Avi's tale is told from the perspective of a malamute named McKinley who is tempted to run off into the wild with a pack of wolves.

These were the first books he bought on his own. Later on, he discovered the English classic *The Wind in the Willows* (1908) by Kenneth Grahame, which he read over and over again, calling it "one of the best books ever written." Set in the English countryside, the novel tells the adventures of Mole, Ratty, Badger, and Toad—all of whom behave very much like humans. Although Avi especially loved the boastful, terribly funny Mr. Toad, he identified with shy and gentle Mole.

In the summertime, while Joseph remained in the city to work, Helen and the three children spent time at rented cottages in the countryside or at the seashore. Later, when Avi was seven, the Wortises purchased an abandoned farmhouse on Shelter Island, at the isolated eastern tip of Long Island, New York. Avi loved the relaxing summers at Shelter Island. It was a great place to read, and its calm, sandy bays were perfect for sailing and swimming. Much later, the island's landscape would inspire the settings for several of Avi's early novels, including *Captain Grey* (1977), *Shadrach's Crossing* (1983; later republished under the title *Smuggler's Island*), and *A Place Called Ugly* (1981). The time he spent sailing is also reflected in his books, including *Windcatcher* (1991). During the summer, he spent time in a one-person sailboat.

He imagined sailing off to islands like those in the novel. "In my head I put together the adventure story of the boy, the boat, and the islands," he states on his website. "But I do have a confession to make: I've never actually been to the Thimble Islands. But then, sometimes imaginary islands are better than the real ones."

CHAPTER TWO

LIVING WITH WAR

When Avi was only four years old, the world changed all around him. Pearl Harbor was attacked on December 7—and the United States entered World War II. When Avi began kindergarten in the fall of 1942, American troops were fighting against Italy, Japan, and Nazi Germany in the name of democracy. The war changed life for the Wortis family in many ways. Joseph Wortis, a psychiatrist, joined the US Navy and was assigned to New York City. He counseled soldiers, many of whom were traumatized by the horrors of the war.

BLACKOUTS AND ID TAGS

As the fighting in the Atlantic grew worse, Americans began to worry that Germany would bomb some of the largest cities on the East Coast, especially New York. As a safety measure, blackouts were often declared.

Blackouts were frightening, especially to young people like Avi. A siren would shriek, and people had to go inside immediately and cover their windows with thick black curtains so that no lights could be seen by enemy bombers. Citizens patrolled the streets to make sure people were following the rules. All of these precautions made the threat of enemy bombers seem very real to Avi.

As an additional precautionary measure, Avi and other children had to wear metal identification tags around their necks. This way, in the event of a bombing, children who were lost or had been injured could be identified and reunited with their parents. On Avi's first-grade report card, he received an S (satisfactory) for "Identification Tag," meaning he was never without his tag. At Avi's public school, first-graders were given one of three types of marks: U (unsatisfactory), I (improved), and S (satisfactory). In first grade, almost every mark Avi received was an S. He did receive a U, though, for "Using a Handkerchief" and "Covering Mouth when Coughing." Apparently, he was not very good at either of these things.

During the war, many products were scarce. Natural resources were needed to build airplanes and ships. There was also a great demand for extra food and clothing for American troops overseas. Because of these shortages, many household items, such as sugar, butter, and fabric, were rationed. Other materials, such as metal and paper, were recycled. Avi did his part to help the war effort. After school, he collected scrap metal and old newspapers for recycling.

There was even a shortage of housing. With so many men and women involved in the war effort, there weren't any workers available to build new homes. Many families who had spare rooms, including Avi's family, took in boarders. One of their boarders was a medical student who kept a human skeleton in his closet.

Life during war was definitely challenging, with moments of fear and nervousness, but it still offered plenty of good times.

BASEBALL GAMES AND CLIFFHANGERS

Until eighth grade, Avi's school was in a residential neighborhood, only a few blocks away from his house. After school, kids got together to play in the street. Although Avi didn't like playing sports, he did love the Brooklyn Dodgers baseball team. He rarely missed the chance to listen to a game on the radio.

Even into the late 1940s, very few people in the United States and Canada had television sets. Instead, the two most popular forms of entertainment were radio and movies. When Avi wasn't reading, he often gathered around the radio with Emily and Henry, listening to radio shows. The three of them loved funny comedians such as Jack Benny and Fred Allen, who were like the Jimmy Fallons of their day. Other favorite radio shows were suspenseful adventure tales featuring superheroes Captain Midnight, the Green Hornet, and Ice Man.

Avi could hardly wait for Saturday mornings because that was when he and his two best friends, Dickie Macht and Phillip Schwartz, spent hours at the local movie theater. Cartoons were followed by one or two full-length westerns. The grand finale was an action-adventure film, with an ending that left the audience in a state of nail-biting suspense. Naturally, the boys had to come back the following Saturday to see how the cliffhanger was resolved.

FINDING INSPIRATION

Avi's childhood was full of inspiring experiences, from food shortages and blackouts to radio shows, comic books, and Saturday movies. Each one of these experiences made it possible for him to view the world as a place filled with stories—stories that could be told in many different ways. Later on, these elements of his life would make their way into his books. For example, nightly radio shows, the war, and even the medical student boarder who kept his skeleton in the closet were all featured in one of the novels Avi has called his most autobiographical, *"Who Was That Masked Man, Anyway?"* (1992).

Set in Brooklyn during World War II, the main character, Frankie, is as obsessed with the fictional heroes on radio shows as many young people today are with video games. In fact, Frankie prefers the fictional radio shows to reality. Along with his timid best friend and next-door neighbor, Mario, Frankie acts out his heroic fantasies. These include spying on the "evil" boarder in Frankie's house and setting up a tin-can walkie-talkie system between their houses. The boys also try to arrange a marriage between Frankie's older brother, Tom, who has come home from the war wounded and depressed, and their sixth-grade teacher, Miss Gomez, a movie star look-alike whose boyfriend was killed overseas. (Like Frankie, young Avi loved to playact and make up stories. He did so with his close friend and cousin Michael Saltz, who lived around the corner and who later inspired the character of Mario.)

The imaginative plot of *"Who Was That Masked Man, Anyway?"* is matched by the inventive way it is told. Instead of chapters, the novel is divided

Earl Grasser voiced the Lone Ranger for Detroit's WXYZ radio. This character inspired Avi to use a quote from the show as his book title: *"Who Was That Masked Man, Anyway?"*

into episodes. Each episode alternates between dialogue and actual fragments of 1940s radio scripts. Adventure shows such as *The Green Hornet* and *The Lone Ranger* are reproduced, commercials and all, just as Frankie and Mario would have

THE WAY YOU LOOK AT THE WORLD

Almost all writers are eventually asked where they find their ideas, and that includes Avi. In a 2003 interview with the New York Public Library, he explained that writers often think differently from other people. As he described it, "Let's imagine a street with trees and cars and houses. If a botanist walked down that street, they would notice mostly the trees—what kind of trees, their age, and maybe the flowers in gardens. An architect walking down that street would notice the trees, but would look at the design of the houses and would probably guess when they were built, things like that. If I were a car mechanic going down that street," he continued, "I would notice the trees and houses, but mostly I'd notice the cars—what kind, how old, unusual cars, and so forth. I'm a storyteller. When I walk down that street, I see stories where other people saw trees or houses or cars. It's the way you look at the world, and a writer is somebody who thinks of stories in terms of words, because there are many ways to tell a story."

heard them. The novel's title is a direct quote of the line spoken at the end of *The Lone Ranger* as the masked cowboy hero and his trusty sidekick, Tonto, rode off into the distance.

Both World War II and Avi's Brooklyn childhood served as the backdrop for the novel *Don't You Know There's a War On?* (2001). The format of this novel, which takes place over a seven-day period in March 1943, is more traditional than *"Who Was That Masked Man, Anyway?"* However, the narrative, which recounts each of the seven days, is preceded by real newspaper headlines announcing events that actually happened on each date. Avi's successful integration of historical fact into the narrative highlights the reality of war. The generous sprinkling of quotes from radio programs, war posters, and cinema newsreels adds to the historically authentic feel of the book.

In the novel, eleven-year-old Howie Crispers worries about his father, who is in the US Marines dodging Nazi warships in the North Atlantic. While his mother works long days at the Navy Yard, Howie is responsible for taking care of his pesky little sister, Gloria. When he complains, his mother, like most other characters in the novel, responds by asking him if he's not aware that there's a war going on.

This novel certainly reflects Avi's childhood experiences. The character Howie goes around the neighborhood with his best friend, Denny, collecting scrap metal, newspapers, and old clothes for the war effort, just as Avi did with his friend. He stays inside during blackouts, uses ration books to buy what little food is in the grocery store, and contents himself with the letters his father sends. These letters resemble swiss cheese when they arrive because so much has been cut out by censors. Of course, Howie and Denny still have fun. Aside from listening to the radio adventures of Captain Midnight and Jack Armstrong, the All-American Boy, they go to Saturday afternoon movies. They also mastermind a scheme to save the job of their much-loved sixth-grade teacher, Miss Gossim, whom both boys have desperate crushes on.

If not for his very own stepson Jack, Avi might not have decided to write this novel. Jack was working on a project about World War II and asked to interview him. "That interview got me thinking about those times, what my life was like, and how we—as kids—learned to deal with the tensions, shortages, struggles to hold life together in those dark days. For better and for worse we did live differently then," he explained to Jack in the interview.

CHAPTER THREE

FINDING HIS WAY

Avi struggled in school, finding it quite boring, so he spent a great deal of his time daydreaming. He often felt like a failure because of his constant battle to get control over his writing. When he was trying to write a paragraph, he might correctly spell a word at the beginning but spell the same word incorrectly a few lines later. So Avi dreaded Friday: the day the class had to take spelling tests. When teachers returned his papers, they were often covered in red marks and corrections. Worst of all, even if Avi was able to grasp his teachers' comments and instructions, there was no way he could be sure he would be able to follow them later on.

Although Avi worked very hard at his writing, his efforts went unnoticed.

Unaware of the seriousness of the problem, Avi's teachers simply thought that he wasn't trying hard enough. The constant criticism Avi received made him angry. Unfortunately, it wasn't until he was in his forties that Avi discovered that there was an actual term for his problem. The frustration with his writing was frequently made worse by the fact that Emily was particularly good at spelling and writing. The twins were always in the same classes during elementary school, which made comparisons even more painful.

Finally, at the end of seventh grade, Avi rebelled. Instead of being in the same eighth-grade class as Emily, he demanded to be assigned to Mr. Malakoski's class. Mr. Mai, as he was called by the students, was a science teacher and Avi loved science. Not only did he receive high marks in the sciences at school, but at home (like Mario in *"Who Was That Masked Man, Anyway?"*), he often read magazines such as *Popular Science* and *Popular Mechanics.*

AN ARTIST OR A PILOT

Aside from science, Avi had a flair for art. The Wortis family recalls coming downstairs for breakfast one day to discover that nine-year-old Avi had sculpted the butter into the shape of a mouse. The only

AVI AND IRVY

At school, Avi's twin sister, Emily, became friends with a girl named Betty Bao. In 1947, Betty had emigrated from China to the United States. Betty grew up to become the author Betty Bao Lord. She went on to write an award-winning book called *In the Year of the Boar and Jackie Robinson* (1984). Two of the characters in the book are actually based on her old childhood friends Avi and Emily. (Avi's name was changed—just a little—to Irvy.) Avi admits that Lord's description of him rings quite true. In addition to being shy, he was fascinated with science (in Lord's book, Irvy can't stop talking about spiders) and was very nervous around girls.

problem was that Avi's dirty hands had turned the butter gray. Avi also liked to draw. Inspired by his science magazines, he took to designing his own airplanes and rockets. For a time, he even considered becoming an aircraft designer.

Apart from designing them, Avi longed to fly the fantastic airplanes he dreamed up. Since that wasn't possible, he did the next best thing—he created

Illustrator Brian Floca autographs his books at BookExpo America. Avi worked with Floca on his novel *City of Light, City of Dark* to create a "comic-book novel."

fictional characters who were able to fly them. When Avi was around ten years old, he wrote a play set in the twenty-second century, featuring an adventurous pilot named Nick Colt. The original manuscript illustrates his struggle with writing. From one page to the next, the word "scene" is alternately spelled "scean," "scenn," "sean," and "seane."

Later, Avi resurrected these childhood fantasies in the novel *City of Light, City of Dark* (1993). Remembering the adventure comics he had read as a boy, Avi teamed up with illustrator Brian Floca and created an original "comic-book novel"—a mixture of narrative, dialogue, and illustrations. Subtitles were provided to translate the Spanish dialogue between main character Carlos Juarez and his mother.

The novel's format and plot were equally imaginative. Set in a futuristic Manhattan, Carlos stumbles upon a magic subway token. Meanwhile, a mysterious parking meter attendant named Asterel and the villainous Thor Underton—a blind man who makes neon signs—are searching for the token. Carlos meets Sarah Stubbs, the daughter of a candy maker, and together the teens discover that the token is the secret supply of power in the city. If, by December 21 at noon, the magic token isn't delivered to the dangerous Kurbs, shadowy spirits who rule over the metropolis, the entire city will freeze over. The characters end up riding in one of the flying machines that Avi had imagined in his childhood.

A PLACE TO BE ALONE

During elementary school, Avi discovered the joys of going to the local library. As he humorously recalls, "No Friday came without a quick trip to the local library. Why quick? Great selection of books. No public toilet." His favorite books at that time were mostly adventure tales such as Robert Louis Stevenson's *Treasure Island* (1883) and Jules Verne's *20,000 Leagues Under the Sea* (1869). In fact, the first time Avi stayed up all night was because he was so caught up in Jules Verne's novel that he couldn't go to sleep. In the meantime, he also began saving

Young Avi enjoyed exploring the local library, discovering authors like Robert Louis Stevenson and Jules Verne. He saved his money to buy books for his very own library.

his allowance to buy books and start his own library.

Today, Avi claims that he learned much more about how to become a writer from all the books he read at home than from anything he was taught in school. Although he got along well with his family, he often felt somewhat distant from them. In these moments, he often turned to books for company. Avi didn't mind being an outsider. Instead, he found that being alone was "enormously appealing." He relished the chance to hang out by himself and read, write, and daydream.

Avi felt as though his parents were far more attentive to his siblings than they were to him. His father seemed like a cold and distant man who never expressed affection. Avi also cannot understand why such well-educated people as his parents never said or did anything about his dyslexia. They knew about the condition but never mentioned it to him or anyone else. It would have helped him understand his struggle—and made his school years an easier time

CHAPTER FOUR

SCHOOL DECISIONS

After his difficult years at PS 8, Avi was ready for something better. He decided to go to Stuyvesant High School in Manhattan. It had a great reputation—especially in science. Best of all, Avi's older brother, Henry, was enrolled there.

But unfortunately, Stuyvesant proved to be a complete catastrophe. An all-boys school at the time, it was so overcrowded that students went to school in two separate shifts. With five thousand students enrolled, it was impossible for teachers to give much of any individual attention to students. Avi was not doing well, but he did not know where to find help. During his first semester, he failed all of his courses, including wood shop.

Avi enrolled at Stuyvesant High School, but the crowded school did not offer the personal attention he needed to succeed. Luckily, he transferred to the writing-focused Elizabeth Irwin High School.

Now what was he to do? Finally, Avi transferred to Elizabeth Irwin High School, a small, coed private school where students received lots of personal attention from teachers. Avi liked this new school much better. However, in contrast to Stuyvesant, Elizabeth Irwin's teachers placed a lot of emphasis on writing. For Avi, writing was still torture. No matter how hard he worked, his assignments were still cluttered with errors. By eleventh grade, most of his teachers had given up on him. Worst of all, Avi had given up on himself.

Then something happened to help Avi. One of his teachers suggested he get a writing tutor. Ella Ratner lived close to Avi's family and was happy to help him out. The first time she and Avi met, Ratner asked to see some of his writing. He showed her a play he had written. After reading it, she turned to him and said, "You're very interesting. You have lots of interesting ideas. If you wrote better, people would know that."

Her positive feedback had a great impression on sixteen-year-old Avi. It was the first time someone had encouraged him as a writer. It filled him with hope and determination. From then on, he didn't care about the red marks all over his compositions or his teachers' criticisms. He continued to write his plays. Influenced by the habits of other writers, he also began to keep a journal. In March 1955, he wrote in its pages, "I can't wait anymore. I'm going to become a playwright."

A SPORTING IDEA

Although he was never very athletic, in high school Avi had his first—and only—experience with team sports when he became captain of the school's soccer team. Although the team lost most of its games, Avi still enjoyed playing. The experience later inspired one of his novels for young people, *S.O.R. Losers* (1984). Reviewed in the *Horn Book Magazine,* an important journal of children's literature, the book was described as "one of the funniest and most original sports sagas [adventures] on record."

In the novel, narrator Ed Sitrow (which is "Wortis" spelled backwards), his best friend, Pete Saltz (named in honor of Avi's friend and cousin Michael Saltz), and nine other seventh graders have successfully managed to avoid all sports throughout their years at school. However, their accomplishments in writing, art, music, and science are clearly not impressing the adults around them. In the name of the school's "fine sports tradition" and the "American [way of] life," they are hunted down and made to join the school's soccer team.

Although they do play, the two boys refuse to get caught up in the pressure to win placed upon them by the school as well as their parents. Instead, they have the time of their lives—by losing game after game. When told by his teacher that "it's important to win," Ed replies with a puzzled, "Why?"

BRINGING BACK OLD FRIENDS

Avi based other stories on his old friends the characters Ed Sitrow and Pete Saltz. They can be found in *Romeo and Juliet—Together (and Alive!) at Last* (1987), a novel based on a situation from Avi's high school years. In the story, Ed is dumbfounded to discover that his pudgy and poetic pal Pete has a crush on the mousy, bookish Anabell Stackpoole. The only problem is that both are too shy even to look at each other. To help matters, Ed and his friends come up with the idea of staging a school production of Shakespeare's *Romeo and Juliet* and casting Pete and Anabell in the lead roles. The book's hilarious events closely mirror Avi's experience when he won the lead part in a senior play and developed a major crush on his costar, Alice.

Unfortunately, unlike Anabell and Pete, Alice was not interested in Avi. In fact, during high school, Avi's boyish features and short height, coupled with his shyness, made it difficult for him to impress girls. He was not terribly pleased when he was voted to make "the best future husband" in his class, but he did like the caption in his yearbook photo. It simply read, "He will be surrounded by books."

SECRETS TO GOOD WRITING

On Avi's website, he donates a page to tips for students who want to become better writers. His number-one suggestion is to read—and then read, and read some more. "The more you read, the better the writer you can be," he says. "You can ***never*** read too much." Naturally, his next piece of advice is to write and then rewrite, admitting that he rewrites his works fifty to sixty times. He adds, "Here's a tip: read your first draft, and if you think it's good, you are in trouble. But, if you read it and you see it's not that good, you are in great shape—to get going. The more you rewrite, the better your writing will be." His final suggestion is to listen. Read your work out loud and listen for what needs to be changed.

CHOOSING A COLLEGE

When it came to make the decision about choosing a college, Avi thought he would like to attend Antioch College in Yellow Springs, Ohio. It was an experimental school and students were given a great deal of freedom. However, the lack of structure was difficult for him, so he transferred to the

Avi majored in history and theater at Madison's University of Wisconsin. He pointedly avoided English classes, even though he was planning to become a playwright.

University of Wisconsin in Madison. He decided to major in both history and theater.

Although he steered clear of English classes, he was still more determined than ever to become a playwright. Every year the university had a playwriting contest. In order to ensure fair judging, students submitted their manuscripts anonymously. In Avi's final year of college, he decided to submit a play he had written. When it was handed back to him, it was accompanied by the judge's comments, "This person is obviously not an English-speaking person, but he is making great strides in learning the language and should be encouraged."

Avi spent an additional year at Wisconsin after his graduation in 1959, doing graduate work in playwriting and submitting a play to the contest again. His fascination with American history resulted in his writing an American Revolution comedy called *A Little Rebellion.* It won the contest and was published in two magazines and staged at the university's theater. A thrilled Avi had proved himself as a writer. Next he needed to figure out if this was a way he could make a living for himself.

CHAPTER FIVE

MARRIAGE AND FATHERHOOD

Avi was ready to make a living as a playwright—but he had no idea how difficult that could be. His new plan started off well. In 1960, he moved to San Francisco. There he was the resident playwright for the World Theater. He continued to write play after play, but there was quite a difference between writing a play and getting it produced on the stage. The theatre was not interested in most of what he wrote, and the one time they liked a play, it never made it from approval to an actual performance.

A NEW START

After a year, Avi became frustrated with the theater scene in San Francisco and decided to try his luck in the theater capital of North America, New York City. Settling in Manhattan, Avi continued to write. However, he wasn't selling any plays, and he needed to pay the rent. To make money, he took any job he could find. He painted signs (complete with spelling mistakes), fried hamburgers, did some carpentry jobs, and worked as an acting coach at a Young Men's Hebrew Association (YMHA) in the Bronx.

At the YMHA, Avi met and fell in love with Joan Gainer, a dance coach. When they began to talk about marriage, Avi began to think about getting a more stable job. One day, wandering around the main New York Public Library Avi discovered a job opening for a clerk for the theater collection. It seemed the perfect job for a playwright who loved being surrounded by books.

Soon after he began work, Avi heard some exciting news. In three years, the library's entire performing arts collection would be moving to its own library, part of a new arts complex called Lincoln Center. In order to increase his chances of getting a good job at the new library, Avi decided he would pursue a master's degree in library science at Columbia University.

For the next three years, Avi worked during the day and went to school at night. Meanwhile,

Avi enjoyed working among so many books as a clerk at the New York Public Library. He later studied library science in hopes of getting a better position.

when time permitted, he continued writing plays—"a trunkful," he admits. "But 99 percent of them weren't any good."

A DIFFERENT APPROACH

When a friend suggested writing a novel instead of more plays, Avi agreed to give it a try. He wrote two adult novels and showed them to his friend. In turn, the friend took the books to a literary agent. The agent tried to sell one of the novels to a publishing house, but the company just was not interested.

In November 1963, Avi and Joan were married. Three years later, Joan gave birth to the couple's first son, Shaun. Avi was thrilled to be a father, but he worried about how he would support his new family on a librarian's low salary. One way he thought up to earn more money was to make and sell greeting cards. A friend had suggested this after receiving a funny card that Avi had illustrated. Although the scheme never worked out, another friend liked Avi's drawings so much that she asked him to provide illustrations for a children's book she was writing.

When the friend submitted the book to a publishing house, the editor who read it didn't like the story, but she loved the drawings. She called Avi and asked if he would be interested in illustrating books. At first, Avi said no. After all, he was a writer, not an illustrator. However, when the editor promised him that he could not only illustrate but also write a book for her, it was a deal that Avi couldn't refuse.

There was only one problem. In a week, Avi, Joan, and Shaun were leaving the country to spend a year in England. Through an exchange program, Avi was going to work at an English library while an English librarian came to work at his job in New

York. How would Avi be able to write and illustrate an entire book in seven days?

Racking his brain for ideas, Avi thought about the bedtime stories he invented for Shaun. Each night he would ask his son what kind of story he wanted to hear, and Shaun would make suggestions such as, "Tell me a story about a glass of water." Avi wrote down a series of these tales and submitted them just as he was about to fly to England.

In the end, the editor who had commissioned the book didn't like the manuscript, but Avi's agent sent it around until he found a publishing house that wanted it. As it happened, the editor who accepted Avi's book liked the stories but didn't think much of the artwork. When *Things That Sometimes Happen* was finally published in 1970, just the text was by Avi; the illustrations were by another artist.

During the publication of this first book, Avi's agent called him to ask what name he wanted to appear on the book. Avi replied, "Oh, just say Avi." From that time on, "Avi" is all he has ever been called by his reading public.

The publication of *Things That Sometimes Happen* was a turning point in Avi's life. He had achieved one of his biggest dreams: He had finally proved himself as a writer. He also realized that he should pursue children's fiction, so he stopped writing adult novels and plays.

As an adult, Avi continued to collect books for his personal library. His collection of historical children's novels was an inspiration for his later writing.

When Avi and Joan returned home from England in 1970, they brought with them their recently born son, Kevin. With two children to support, Avi began looking around for a better-paying job. Almost immediately he found one as a librarian at Trenton State College, in New Jersey.

The family moved to Trenton and life became very busy. Avi was working full-time as a librarian and continued writing new books whenever he could. Later, he began teaching children's literature at the college. He began collecting rare first editions of children's books that he found at garage sales and secondhand stores. Many times he paid less than a dollar for these literary treasures. Before long, he owned more than three thousand books!

Avi collected children's books from all periods, but he particularly enjoyed older and historical novels. Later in his career, when he began writing novels for middle school and young adult readers, his book collection was a source of inspiration for the style, language, settings, and descriptive details of his own "historical" tales.

A GROWING AUDIENCE

Avi loved being a father and spending time with his sons, Shaun and Kevin. He particularly enjoyed reading to them—both his own books and those of

FROM WORDS TO ILLUSTRATIONS

Avi's series about Poppy has entertained and delighted readers of all ages for years. The illustrations in those books are the handiwork of illustrator Brian Floca. It is his talent that brings Avi's words to life in soft, engaging illustrations. Floca has earned many different awards for his art, including a Caldecott Medal in 2014. In addition to illustrating the Poppy series, Floca also drew the pictures in Avi's *City of Light, City of Dark*. On Avi's blog, he recalls meeting Floca for the first time. He was looking for an artist to help him create the graphic novel style of the book. He was introduced to Brian Floca. "Brian and I met over a period of years to create *City of Light, City of Dark*," he wrote on January 7, 2014. "It [the book] is still around and still enjoyed. And Brian is still traveling fast."

other authors. He claims that he learned more from these reading sessions than his sons did. Through their reaction to various stories, he discovered how kids react to various books: what they like, what they don't like, how to amuse them and scare them, and how to grab their attention and hold on to it throughout the length of a book.

Perhaps not surprisingly, as Shaun and Kevin grew older, so did the audience Avi wrote for. His first book, *Things That Sometimes Happen,* was a picture book for toddlers, and *Snail Tale* was for young readers. *No More Magic* and subsequent novels were aimed at middle school children. Then in 1981, Avi published *A Place Called Ugly,* his first young adult novel. He remembers quite well how the idea for the story came to him. "Once upon a time—it was the last day of a Labor Day weekend—I was about to drive my family home. We had been visiting with my parents. My son Kevin had been complaining about going back to school. Then, just as we were getting into the car, ready to go, he vanished. My first thought was, 'Oh oh, Kevin is hiding so he can stay with his grandparents and miss school.' My second thought was, 'Hey, that's a good idea for a story.'"

The novel begins with fourteen-year-old Owen's parents leaving him behind at the end of the summer. Only, unlike Kevin, who only left the car to go to the bathroom, Owen refuses to leave his family's "ugly," old, broken-down summer cottage. Threatened by real estate developers who want to bulldoze it to the ground in order to build a luxury hotel, Owen is determined to fight so that things can remain the same.

In this book, Avi tackled one of his favorite themes: a young person who discovers his or her identity by questioning and even fighting adult authority. Following *A Place Called Ugly*, Avi has alternated between writing for middle school and young adult audiences. But the theme of kids challenging adults remained constant in all his books.

In 1976, Avi, Joan, and the boys moved from New Jersey to New Hope, Pennsylvania. The family lived there until Avi and Joan separated in 1982. By then, the boys were almost grown. Shaun went off to college, and Avi moved to a house where he could be near Kevin, who lived with Joan.

Not long after Avi's divorce from Joan, his sister, Emily, introduced him to Coppelia Kahn, someone she knew from college. Coppelia had recently divorced as well. She taught college literature and had a son named Gabriel. Avi and Coppelia liked each other immediately, and soon they were talking about getting married. When Coppelia was offered a job at Brown University in Providence, Rhode Island, the two moved. The move inspired Avi to make another big decision: he would no longer look for work as a librarian. Instead, he would put all of his time and attention on making a living as an author.

CHAPTER SIX

BRINGING HISTORY TO LIFE

For an author interested in writing historical stories, Providence was a wonderful place to live. The city's history dated back to 1636 and was brimming with all kinds of imagination-inspiring colonial buildings and landmarks. Avi had had a love of history since he was a child, so he was delighted with his new home.

Some of Avi's earliest memories were of his relatives', especially his grandfather's, early American history discussions. His special interest in the American Revolution had led Avi to major in history at the University of Wisconsin. It wasn't long before it found its way into his novels for young people.

HISTORICAL TALES

Captain Grey, Night Journeys (1979), *Encounter at Easton* (1980), *The Fighting Ground* (1984), and *Sophia's War: A Tale of the Revolution* (2012) take place in the period around the American Revolution. The war against the British monarchy provides a perfect backdrop for these novels in which orphaned American children are forced to rebel against adult rules and authority figures to stay alive.

Night Journeys and its sequel, *Encounter at Easton,* were both set in the vicinity of New Hope, Pennsylvania, in the year 1768, just before the Revolutionary War. *Night Journeys* begins when recently orphaned twelve-year-old Peter York is taken in by a Quaker family. When two runaway indentured servants escape, Peter begs his guardian to let him join the search party. He longs to earn the reward offered for their recapture. However, he is conflicted when he discovers that the runaways are children close to his own age. Suddenly, all he can think about is outwitting the adults around him in order to help the children escape. That escape and the continued pursuit of the two runaways is continued in the highly suspenseful *Encounter at Easton*.

One of the two runaways resurfaces years later in *Captain Grey.* Set in 1783, the adolescent hero of *Encounter at Easton* has grown to be a mysterious but brutal pirate—Captain Grey—who kidnaps a recently orphaned eleven-year-old named Kevin. Described by a reviewer in the *New York Times Book Review* as "a robust [rich] pirate adventure with a neat twist," *Captain Grey* details how Kevin copes with being kidnapped by a lawless group of pirates, all the while trying to free himself and be reunited with his older sister, Cathleen.

Captain Grey is set in the New Jersey wilderness, close to the city of Trenton, where Avi had lived and taught and also where *The Fighting Ground* was set. *The Fighting Ground* takes place during the war itself, over an emotional, action-packed twenty-four-hour period in April 1778. When a bell tolls, calling civilians to take up arms against the enemy, thirteen-year-old Jonathan mistakes his father's antiwar stance for cowardice. Dying to fight, he runs off to enlist. However, out on the battlefield, things are far from glamorous. The battle is difficult and bloody, and the corporal Jonathan looked up to reveals himself to be a cruel manipulator. Having discovered that he himself is a coward and that war is hell, Jonathan returns home to his father, alive, but forever changed.

Critics praised this book greatly. Writing in the *Bulletin of the Center for Children's Books,* Zena Sutherland applauded the novel for making "war personal and immediate; not history or event, but experience; near and within oneself, and horrible." As with many of Avi's historical novels, the setting and details are rooted in the past. At the same time, young people can clearly identify with characters whose dilemmas are timeless and universal. Among the numerous awards bestowed upon *The Fighting Ground* was the 1985 Scott O'Dell Award for historical fiction. O'Dell himself, a famous writer of historical fiction for young people, singled Avi out as a talented writer, one who he said was "keep[ing] historical fiction alive" for young people.

In *Sophia's War*, the main character becomes a spy and the book centers on concepts of treason, justice, and revenge. *School Library Journal* wrote, "*Sophia's War* is outstanding historical fiction, bringing to dramatic life the human story behind extraordinary events."

A HISTORICAL FRAMEWORK

As Avi himself confesses, "Somewhere along the line, I can't explain where, I developed an understanding of history not as fact but as story." History provides a framework that Avi uses to tell a really good story in a new, challenging way.

For instance, both *Emily Upham's Revenge; or, How Deadwood Dick Saved the Banker's Niece: A Massachusetts Adventure* (1978) and *The History of Helpless Harry: To Which Is Added a Variety of Amusing and Entertaining Adventures* (1980) stemmed from Avi's considerable knowledge of the history of children's literature. Both stories were set in the Victorian period (1875 and 1845, respectively). They were also written in the literary tradition of that era, a period in which books for young readers were often overly sentimental and very moralistic. By imitating and comically exaggerating situations, viewpoints, vocabulary, mannerisms, and even book titles of the mid- to late 1800s, Avi crafted two books that were entertaining while poking fun at social conventions and attitudes that are still in existence today.

Later, in 1996, he returned once again to Victorian literature. The result was *Beyond the Western Sea,* a two-volume epic novel in the spirit of English writer Charles Dickens. One of the world's great novelists, and Avi's all-time favorite authors, Dickens was renowned for novels such as *Oliver Twist* (1838), *Great Expectations* (1859), and *A Tale of Two Cities* (1861). Like Dickens's sweeping novels, *Beyond the Western Sea* featured a huge cast of characters and short chapters, each of which ended with a breathtaking cliffhanger. Plots were filled with chance meetings, narrow escapes, and surprising revelations.

Critics mostly praised what one reviewer for the *Horn Book Magazine* called a "rip-roaring

AN ONGOING TRADITION

Avi's love of history and drive to create intriguing historical fiction has continued over the years. In *Hard Gold* (2009), he explores life during the gold rush of 1859 and the difficult journey west. *Kirkus Reviews* stated, "What will make this interesting for readers who like action is the relentless foreshadowing of evil and heartbreak, the short chapters, the trademark Avi cliffhangers, sharp attention to interesting (but not overwhelming) historical detail and the many period illustrations and photographs."

In *City of Orphans* (2012), he focuses on the newsboys and gangs of 1893. His character Maks Geless is a young newsboy and sometime detective coping with life in the tenements of New York. *Kirkus Reviews* says, "Heroic deeds, narrow escapes, dastardly villains, amazing coincidences and a family rich in love and hope are all part of an intricate and endlessly entertaining adventure."

As Avi writes on his website, "Dates are interesting—it's helpful to know when things happened—but it's the stories of people doing the most amazing things, things that often change the world, that grab my imagination."

rollercoaster ride" about a pair of poor Irish siblings in the 1850s, who, together with the son of their wealthy landlord, run off to Liverpool and board a ship bound for America. Avi himself admits that the fourteen-hour days he put into writing the two-volume novel made it the most difficult book he has written to date.

THE CITIES' HISTORIES

For Avi, writing historical fiction consists of more than describing facts and events of the past. Equally important is the choice of a convincing historical setting, or location. When he moves to a new city, Avi always tries to learn everything he can about its history. Actually being in a place allows him to visualize its past and create a believable setting. For example, first New Jersey and then Pennsylvania provided the backdrops for most of his earlier historical novels. And when he settled in Providence, the history of Rhode Island's capital became central to his fiction.

Wondering about the former occupants of the old house where he and his wife were living led Avi to write *Something Upstairs* (1988). The novel begins when a twelve-year-old boy named Kenny moves into an eighteenth-century Providence

Although books like *Something Upstairs* focus on serious subjects like slavery, Avi also thinks it's important to include humor in his books to help children learn.

house (modeled on Avi's own home) and meets a ghost. Only this particular ghost is a young slave boy named Caleb who was murdered in 1800. As Kenny travels back in time with Caleb to help solve his murder, Avi contrasts Providence of the past with the present-day city. Although Kenny's ability to travel through time adds an element of fantasy to the novel, it also exposes a theme that is important to Avi: history is not dead. Instead, as memory, it is always a living part of the present.

A measure of the success of *Something Upstairs* was that the Providence Preservation Society began including Avi's (and Kenny's) house on its guided historical tours of the city. Other monuments on the tour were featured in another novel of Avi's, *The Man Who Was Poe* (1989).

Written in a style that mimicked the atmospheric mysteries of the real-life writer Edgar Allan Poe, *The Man Who Was Poe* was described by critic Roger Sutton as a "complex, atmospheric thriller." Set in 1848, the novel begins when young Edmund and his twin sister arrive in Providence from England with their Auntie Pru, in search of their missing mother. When his aunt and then his sister disappear, Edmund has nobody to turn to—except for the cranky, unpredictable, and alcoholic poet Edgar Allan Poe, whom Avi admired and said was an "incredible and complex figure."

In *The Man Who Was Poe*, Avi mixes nonfiction and fantasy to create a gripping thriller in which the readers learn about Providence, Rhode Island, and poet Edgar Allan Poe.

Posing as Auguste Dupin, a fictional detective from the series of Paris mysteries he wrote, Poe agrees to help Edmund unravel the mysteries of his relatives' disappearances. However, his real motivation is to use Edmund's situation as material for a novel he is writing. This creates conflict between the two. Edmund wants nothing more than to be reunited with his family. However, death-obsessed Poe hopes that Edmund's vanished relatives will turn up dead, providing a more interesting ending for his book.

Avi's ability to mix real Providence history and actual people (Poe) with fantasy and fictional characters (Poe's creation Dupin) creates a successful and fascinating novel. Avi's ability to combine history and fantasy shows readers that sometimes the boundaries between true and invented events can be shadowy.

CHAPTER SEVEN

AND JUSTICE FOR ALL

When Avi was writing *The Man Who Was Poe,* his mind kept returning to the story's ship, the *Seahawk*, which became the setting for *The True Confessions of Charlotte Doyle* (1990), his next novel. Although this book had a lot in common with Avi's previous historical novels, it was the novel that would truly change Avi's life as an author forever. This book would win an amazing number of awards and honors between 1990 and 1992.

CHARLOTTE'S STORY

Set in 1832, *The True Confessions of Charlotte Doyle* tells the story of a thirteen-year-old girl from Providence who finds herself alone and trying to survive in a complicated adult world. While Charlotte's well-to-do family isn't dead, they abandon her in England so that she can finish her schooling. Embarking alone—the only child and the only female—on a ship bound for America, the ladylike Charlotte is initially disgusted by the brutish behavior of the crew. When Zachariah, the black cook, makes attempts to befriend her, Charlotte, true to the racist conventions of her day, recoils. Instead, she seeks the companionship and protection of authoritarian Captain Jaggery, whose fine clothes and gentlemanly manners remind her of her father.

It isn't long, however, before Charlotte discovers that the crew is justified in planning an uprising against the cruel and vicious captain. Subsequently forced to question the values of her privileged background, Charlotte rebels against everything she was brought up to be. She discards her fancy dresses, chops off her ringlets, and sets to work on the ship. Branded "an unnatural girl" by the captain, she is determined to prove herself as one of the crew. By exhibiting her courage and physical stamina, she ultimately wins their trust and friendship. In doing so, she discovers her own identity.

In fact, when she finally arrives home in Providence, Charlotte finds that she can no longer be her former self. When her strict father calls her unnatural, burns the journal containing her

The True Confessions of Charlotte Doyle takes readers back to the nineteenth century, when Charlotte is determined to prove a girl can work on a ship, too.

adventures, and confined her to her room, she realizes that, to be true to herself, she has only one option. And so, she returns to the *Seahawk* and the crew that has become her real family.

The novel received praises for its fast-paced plot and attention to historical detail (including appendices with detailed descriptions of a nineteenth-century ship). But what perhaps registered most with readers and critics alike—the book won many awards, including a prestigious Newbery Honor—was the elaboration of one of Avi's most important and ever-present themes. In Charlotte Doyle's transformation, Avi showed that in order to grow up, children often need to rebel against the adult rules that supposedly protect them and challenge those adult values that may turn out to be unjust.

In the acceptance speech he gave when the novel won the Boston Globe/Horn Book Award for fiction, Avi began with a humorous tale about a conversation with a film producer who wanted to adapt *The True Confessions of Charlotte Doyle* into a movie. The producer wanted to change one thing about the story—the ending. She felt that Charlotte's leaving home would encourage kids to become runaways. Avi didn't agree, and he told the producer that she had "the wrong Charlotte." Because they couldn't reach an agreement about this matter, the film was never made.

Luckily, other readers had more inspiring reactions to what children's literature professor and critic Catherine Mercier calls the novel's "improbable but deeply satisfying conclusion." In his acceptance speech, Avi talked about some of the comments that had meant the most to him. There was the eleven-year-old boy in a ninja T-shirt who worried that Charlotte was "going to have a hard time getting married." There was also a woman who told Avi that she finished the book in tears—tears of relief that Charlotte had the courage to follow her own path. Best of all was the eleven-year-old Seattle girl who wrote Avi a letter to say, "Charlotte lives in my heart! Forever!" Said Avi, "If the 'improbable' life I wrote lives in someone's heart as a life possible, then I have already been given the greatest gift a writer can receive."

AN ACT OF DEFIANCE

The year after publishing *The True Confessions of Charlotte Doyle,* Avi had another great success— and won a second Newbery Honor—with a completely different novel entitled *Nothing but the Truth.* Set in the contemporary United States, the story revolves around ninth-grader Philip Malloy. When poor marks in English keep him off the track team, Philip takes out his resentment on his teacher Miss Narwin by humming along loudly during the playing of the "Star-Spangled Banner," which is against school rules. The style of the novel was quite a departure for Avi. It was written in documentary style, with memos, diary excerpts, transcripts, and letters.

Although Miss Narwin likes Philip, she sends him to the principal for disrupting class. When he disrupts the class again by loudly singing along with the anthem and refuses to apologize, he is suspended. Furious with Miss Narwin, Philip complains to his parents. Though wrapped up in their own problems, they are nonetheless outraged that their son has been suspended for what they view as patriotism—singing the national anthem. Local school board officials and the media are also horrified. They get wind of Philip's story and repeat various, conflicting versions of it, without any regard for the truth.

And just what is the truth? It is a question that Avi raises again and again in his novels. In *Nothing but the Truth,* however, the complicated notion of truth takes center stage. Instead of telling the story from one or even multiple points of view, this realistic "documentary" novel provides the reader with various pieces of evidence. Phone conversations, school memos, letters, and newspaper articles all relate the conflict between Philip and Miss Narwin. It is up to the reader to gather the evidence and judge the truths being told as well as the motives of the tellers. As the title hints, is it really possible to "tell the truth, the whole truth, and nothing but the truth"?

Ultimately, both Philip and Miss Narwin become victims of the so-called truth. As their original conflict becomes blown out of proportion by complete strangers, both become isolated. Abandoned by her colleagues and school authorities, Miss Narwin is forced to leave school. So is Philip, who is misunderstood by his parents, hated by the kids at school, and turned into a poster boy for patriotism by exploitative politicians and complete strangers.

A VARIETY OF GENRES

Avi's books cover a huge variety of genres. While many of his titles are focused on historical periods, from medieval times to the Victorian era to the American Revolution, others are short story collections, thrillers, or suspenseful mysteries. When the New York Public Library asked Avi during an interview if there was any genre that he hadn't written in but might like to try, he talked about how he hadn't written any science fiction and wasn't sure if he would, pointing out that he thought one had to know a lot about science to successfully do that sort of writing. The cowboy story, however, was a genre he was interested in trying out someday. Ultimately, he explained, he'd most like to try writing a western.

A LOSS OF INNOCENCE

A realistic view of social injustice is yet another major theme that Avi is intensely interested in. Early on in his life, Avi became aware of the fact that there were many social inequalities in the world. During the 1930s and 1940s, the Wortis family was politically active. They spoke out against racism and supported increased rights for both women and workers. At the time, such views were considered radical, or extreme, by average Americans. As a result, during his youth, Avi was made to feel like an outsider in some social circles.

In many of his books, Avi's youthful heroes and heroines identify injustice and take on the adult authorities and institutions that defend it. For Avi, childhood is a time of innocence, and children often see the adult world with critical eyes. In all of Avi's novels, young people come into contact and conflict with the adult world. For example, Kenny in *Something Upstairs* takes on racism in the form of slavery, while Charlotte in *The True Confessions of Charlotte Doyle* battles for the rights of women (like herself) and workers (the brutalized, overworked crew). Ida in *The Secret School* (2001) fights for children's right to education, while Owen in *A Place Called Ugly* takes on greedy real estate developers. In *Catch You Later, Traitor* (2015), twelve-year-old Peter Collison deals with the accusation of being a Communist and the damages of the country's Red Scare in the early 1950s.

Often in these books, characters are faced with challenging events through which they lose their childlike innocence. These tough challenges have a benefit, however. The children come through the experiences as bolder, shrewder, more knowledgeable, and more sympathetic adults. Occasionally,

Avi's books have faced the criticism that his themes are undermining adult authority and encouraging young people to be rebellious, but Avi thinks such ideas are a necessary part of children's books. "More than anything else, children's literature is about the place and role of the child in society . . . If we—in the world of children's literature—can help the young stand straight for a moment longer than they would have in the past, help them maintain their ideas and values . . . help them demand—and win—justice, we've added something good to the world," he explained in the *Horn Book Magazine*.

CHAPTER EIGHT

FINDING INSPIRATION AND IDEAS

In 1995, it was time for another move. Avi and his wife Coppelia had divorced, so the author moved to Colorado. In Denver, he was closer to nature, surrounded by mountains and streams. He also relished the abundant sunshine there. Later, he married once more, this time a publisher named Linda Wright. Together, they are parents of a "blended family" of five children.

It comes as no surprise that local geography and history have been featured in several of Avi's novels. *The Good Dog, Perloo the Bold* (1998) and *The Secret School* all have Colorado's mountains as their backdrop.

Avi has been inspired by Colorado's Rocky Mountains and sunshine. When he heads outside for a run, the time away from the keyboard helps him work out plot problems.

EVERYDAY EVENTS AS STORIES

In Colorado, Avi wakes up early and is usually at his computer writing by 6 a.m. He often writes for ten or even twelve hours a day, although he usually takes time out to go for a run. Running not only gets Avi out of the house and provides physical activity, but it just so happens it is also an important part of his writing process. While running, he tries to resolve problems he might be having with the plot of a book.

Avi gets his ideas for his novels and stories from many different sources. In fact, Avi has trained himself to see the everyday events around him as stories. Of these stories in his head, only a fraction are actually considered for a possible book. "I can make up a story about anything," says Avi. "That doesn't mean they are all good. But if I have the basis for a story, I can make it good if I choose to."

Sometimes, one event inspires a story. *Wolf Rider* (1985), for example, is based on an anonymous phone call Avi received from a man who claimed to have murdered a woman. Avi kept the man on the phone while the police tried, unsuccessfully, to trace the call. Although the police told Avi that it was probably a crank call, he couldn't follow their advice and forget about it. He found the woman's name in a phone book and called her to tell her she might be in danger. When he later told a journalist this story, the journalist warned Avi not to get involved or the police would end up thinking that he was the caller.

Other times, a combination of events, conversations, memories, and things he has read snowball, over time, into the beginnings of a book. The idea for *Sometimes I Think I Hear My Name* (1982) was triggered by a series of comments Avi overheard. First, there was a remark about the living situation of a teen Avi knew. Then there was a conversation that Avi had with his wife about teens. Then there was a friend's remark about a certain parent and a quotation from a mystery writer that Avi couldn't get out of his head. All of these elements stuck in Avi's brain and inspired him to sit down and begin writing a novel about thirteen-year-old Conrad Murray, who sneaks off to New York to pay surprise visits to the parents who abandoned him.

The Barn (2014) was based on a combination of memories of his grandfather and spotting an old barn while Avi was on vacation in Northern California. He stopped to take a photo and a woman from a house nearby came out to tell him

After spotting a barn during a California vacation, Avi was inspired to write his novella, *The Barn*. He also used some memories of his grandfather to write this story.

the story behind it. *The Barn* is a novella, and Avi says on his website, "I will confess to believing *The Barn* is as good, if not better, than anything I have ever written."

Once the ideas come, Avi must organize them into a structured story. When he was in school, one of his teachers taught him that the key to writing a play was to start with a written outline of main events. Avi still does this, only now he makes up the outlines in his head instead of writing them out. He considers them the maps that allow him to advance from one part of the story to the next. These story outlines usually change. In fact, Avi often lets the plot events shuffle around in his head for as long as months or even years before he feels ready to begin writing.

In the meantime, he begins researching the story's background. As a former librarian and history lover, this is one part of being a novelist that he really enjoys. Research means not only reading books about other historical periods (the American Revolution, medieval England) or specific subjects (nineteenth-century ships, Edgar Allan Poe), but also looking at photographs, costumes, and illustrations so that he can visualize specific elements.

FROM BEGINNING TO END

Once he is finally ready to start writing, he turns on his computer and begins on the first line of the first page. Avi considers the opening of a book crucial. He feels that the first page is where young readers decide whether they want to continue reading or put the book down.

He writes the first sentence and then rewrites it until he is satisfied. He does the same with the first paragraph, the first page, and the first chapter. When he gets to the end of the first chapter, he goes back to rewrite the beginning—not only the chapter, but the entire book!

Working from the beginning, Avi rarely considers the end until he gets to it. As he confesses, "I rewrite the book at this stage maybe forty or fifty times. Over and over again. I have only the vaguest sense of what I'm doing, and I certainly do not have an ending in mind." While writing, Avi often takes notes about characters. Sometimes he creates whole character descriptions, which he keeps beside him, to glance at when he needs to enter into a character's head. As he says, "Often I go through several drafts before I undertake to describe the characters physically—it takes time to get to know them."

REWRITING AND REREADING

Avi usually finishes his entire first draft of a book quite rapidly. He claims that most of his first drafts are so awful he wouldn't even show them to his cat, let alone a human being. Yet a rough draft provides the blueprint for the real work, which is endless writing and rewriting. For this reason, Avi considers himself a very slow worker.

Avi believes that rereading is as important as rewriting. In his opinion, you cannot be a good writer without first being a good reader. Being an attentive reader allows him to spot problems and make necessary changes to the story.

Having dysgraphia means that Avi can read a passage many times without catching glaring errors. For example, he may write "chess" when he meant "cheese" and discover this mistake months later. To help focus on errors, Avi often reads text out loud.

"Writing is hard for me," he admits. "I love it, but I'm not a natural writer. I don't know who is. I think writing is hard for everyone."

During revisions, Avi counts on the opinions of other readers as well. Particularly important are suggestions made by his agent and his editors. He also seeks feedback from the audience he's writing for—kids. An important part of Avi's career as a writer is the visits he makes to schools and libraries throughout the country. Often he reads manuscripts he is working on. As he says about these visits, "I think it's very important for me to keep these kids in front of my eyes. They're wonderfully interesting and they hold me to the reality of who they are."

How does Avi know when he's finished a book? One of three things usually occurs. Sometimes, he realizes that the changes he's making are so minor—for example, moving a word from one place to another—that they don't make a difference. Other times, his editor calls him up and tells him he has to submit the manuscript because it's going to press. And once in a while, Avi decides a book is finished because he can't stand looking at it anymore.

In terms of the overall time it takes to write a book, it varies greatly. Avi wrote the first draft of *S.O.R. Losers* in one day, but it took him fourteen years to finish *Bright Shadow* (1985). "I would say that on the average, it takes about one and a half years to write a book," Avi told the New York Public Library in an interview, "but sometimes longer and sometimes shorter."

Once Avi is content with a final manuscript, it goes to the editor at the publishing house. Even after it has been written and edited, a book may end up not being published. An editor might decide the book isn't good for some reason. Avi might agree or disagree with the editor's decision. If he really believes in the book, he will send it to other publishers, who might accept it.

WORDCRAFT

Like many people, from students and grandparents to celebrities and authors, Avi has his own blog. Called *Wordcraft*, the blog gives insight into Avi's thoughts, ideas, concerns, and writing process. Readers can search under dozens and dozens of tags or search by clicking on any of twenty-five categories. In a recent post about dealing with first drafts, he wrote, "When I achieve what I call a first draft of a new book—which I have just done—I am flooded with relief. It seems as if a miracle has happened." He compares the writing process to running downhill from a mountain. To read more about Avi's life, check out *Wordcraft* at http://www.avi-writer.com/blog/.

TIME FOR REVIEWS

After publication come the reviews. Historically, Avi has a problem with reviewers. He believes that many do not treat children's literature as a serious form of literature. He is also critical of the actual reviews, which generally limit themselves to a paragraph summing up the plot followed by one or two sentences in which the reviewer judges the book as good or bad. Nevertheless, Avi reads reviews of his books, even though negative ones may upset him.

Although Avi doesn't care enormously about awards, he admits that they have been important to his success as a writer. Winning Newbery Honors for *The True Confessions of Charlotte Doyle* and *Nothing but the Truth* did a lot for Avi's popularity with readers, teachers, and critics. Before the awards, all of Avi's books had gone out of print. Afterward, all except for his two earliest books were republished in paperback editions. Avi's novels became regulars on teachers' reading lists. Meanwhile, in critics' eyes, Avi came to be considered one of the most important writers of children's literature today, a view reconfirmed by his recent Newbery Medal for *Crispin: The Cross of Lead.* The two sequels, *Crispin at the Edge of the World* and *Crispin: The End of Time* have also earned high praise from reviewers.

Avi loves to speak to children, but his special favorite is when he can talk to kids who have learning disabilities, like he did.

No matter how many awards he receives, Avi always secretly fears that his next book will be a failure. However, it is this very fear that keeps him striving to make each book the best it can be.

Through Avi's novels, readers are introduced to worlds where other young people have to battle against very adult complications to reach their targets. But it's Avi's own life story that encourages kids to pursue whatever they want in life. After all, Avi proved he could be a writer and an incredibly successful one. This message is one that Avi wants to share when he visits schools and libraries. It is not unusual for him to ask to speak to kids who have been labeled as learning disabled. He knows just what will happen when they first come into the room, too. "They come in slowly, waiting for yet another pep talk, more instructions. Eyes cast down, they won't even look at me. Their anger glows. I don't say a thing," he says. "I lay out pages of my copy-edited manuscripts, which are covered with red marks. 'Look here,' I say, 'see that spelling mistake. There, another spelling mistake. Looks like I forgot to put a capital letter there. Oops! Letter reversal.' Their eyes lift. They are listening." And Avi knows his friends surround him.

ON AVI

Full name: Edward Irving Wortis

Pen name: His sister, Emily, called him Avi.

Birth date: December 23, 1937

Birthplace: New York, New York

Raised in: Brooklyn, New York

Mother: Helen, a social worker

Father: Joseph, a psychiatrist

Siblings: Emily (twin sister) and Henry (elder brother)

Relatives: One grandfather was a professional storyteller; one grandfather was a romance novel author; one grandmother was a playwright; one aunt was a journalist.

Current residence: Clark, Colorado

Age he decided to become an author: As a high school senior

Previous occupation: Librarian

First writing career: Playwright

First published book: *Things That Sometimes Happen* (1970)

First novel: *No More Magic* (1975)

Recent novel: *Catch You Later, Traitor* (2015)

Marital status: Married Joan Gainer (1963–1982); Coppelia Kahn (1983–1995?); now married to Linda C. Wright

Children: Shaun Wortis, Kevin Wortis, Hayden Kalin, Catherine Wortis, Robert Wortis, Jack Spina, and stepchild Gabriel Kahn

School life: Difficult due to signs of dyslexia

Universities attended: University of Wisconsin; Columbia University

Degrees: BA in history (1959) and MA in drama (1962) from the University of Wisconsin and MS in library science (1964) from Columbia

Awards: Newbery Award, two Newbery Honors, two Horn Book awards, and a Scott O'Dell Award for Historical Fiction

Primary writing goal: To tell a good story

Favorite book: The next one

Research technique: Avi often reads two hundred or more books about history in order to write authentically about a time period.

Writing tip for kids: Write what you would enjoy reading. You'll have more fun, and it will be better.

Hobby: Photography

Member: PEN, Authors Guild

Facebook page: Facebook.com/avi.writer

Twitter: @avi3writer

Personal blog: http://www.avi-writer.com/blog/

ON AVI'S WORK

Abigail Takes the Wheel. New York, NY: HarperCollins, 1999.

Amanda Joins the Circus, New York, NY: HarperCollins, 1999.

The Barn. New York, NY: Orchard Books, 1994.

A Beginning, a Muddle, and an End: The Right Way to Write Writing. Orlando, FL: Harcourt, 2008.

Best Shorts: Favorite Short Stories for Sharing. Boston, MA: Houghton Mifflin, 2006.

Beyond the Western Sea. Book One: The Escape from Home. Book Two: Lord Kirkle's Money. New York, NY: Orchard Books, 1996.

Blue Heron. New York, NY: Bradbury, 1992.

Book Without Words: A Fable of Medieval Magic. New York, NY: Hyperion, 2005.

Bright Shadow. New York, NY: Bradbury, 1985.

Captain Grey. New York, NY: Pantheon, 1977.

Catch You Later, Traitor. Chapel Hill, NC: Algonquin Books, 2015.

The Christmas Rat. New York, NY: Atheneum Books for Young Readers, 2000.

City of Light, City of Dark: A Comic Book Novel. New York, NY: Orchard Books, 1993.

City of Orphans. New York, NY: Atheneum Books for Young Readers, 2012.

Crispin at the Edge of the World. New York, NY: Hyperion, 2006.

Crispin: The Cross of Lead. New York, NY: Hyperion, 2002.

Crispin: The End of Time. New York, NY: Balzer and Bray, 2010.

Devil's Race. New York, NY: HarperTrophy, 1984.

Don't You Know There's a War On? New York, NY: HarperCollins, 2001.

Emily Upham's Revenge; or, How Deadwood Dick Saved the Banker's Niece: A Massachusetts Adventure. New York, NY: Pantheon, 1978.

Encounter at Easton. New York, NY: Pantheon, 1980.

The End of the Beginning: Being the Adventures of a Small Snail (and an Even Smaller Ant). Orlando, FL: Harcourt, 2004.

Ereth's Birthday. New York, NY: HarperCollins, 2000.

The Fighting Ground. New York, NY: Lippincott, 1984.

Finding Providence. New York, NY: HarperCollins, 1997.

The Good Dog. New York, NY: Atheneum Books for Young Readers, 2001.

Hard Gold: The Colorado Gold Rush of 1859. New York, NY: Hyperion, 2008.

The History of Helpless Harry: To Which Is Added a Variety of Amusing and Entertaining Adventures. New York, NY: Pantheon, 1980.

Iron Thunder: The Battle Between the Monitor *and the* Merrimac. New York, NY: Hyperion, 2007.

Keep Your Eye on Amanda. New York, NY: HarperCollins, 1996.

Man from the Sky. New York, NY: Knopf, 1980.

The Man Who Was Poe. New York, NY: Orchard Books, 1989.

The Mayor of Central Park. New York, NY: HarperCollins, 2003.

Midnight Magic. New York, NY: Scholastic, 1999.

Murder at Midnight. New York, NY: Scholastic, 2009.

Never Mind! A Twin Novel. New York, NY: HarperCollins, 2005.

Night Journeys. New York, NY: Pantheon, 1979.

No More Magic. New York, NY: Pantheon, 1975.

Nothing but the Truth. New York, NY: Orchard Books, 1991.

Perloo the Bold. New York, NY: Scholastic, 1999.

A Place Called Ugly. New York, NY: Pantheon, 1981.

Poppy. New York, NY: Orchard, 1995.

Poppy and Ereth. New York, NY: HarperCollins, 2009.

Poppy and Rye. New York, NY: Avon Books, 1998.

Poppy's Return. New York, NY: HarperCollins, 2005.

Prairie School. New York, NY: HarperCollins, 2001.

Punch with Judy. New York, NY: Bradbury, 1993.

Ragweed. New York, NY: Avon Books, 1999.

Romeo and Juliet—Together (And Alive!) at Last. New York, NY: Orchard Books, 1987.

The Secret School. San Diego, CA: Harcourt, 2001.

The Seer of Shadows. New York, NY: HarperCollins, 2008.

Shadrach's Crossing. New York, NY: Pantheon, 1983.

Silent Movie. New York, NY: Atheneum/Anne Schwartz Books, 2003.

Smuggler's Island. New York, NY: HarperCollins, 1994.

Snail Tale: The Adventures of a Rather Small Snail.

New York, NY: Pantheon, 1972.

Something Upstairs. New York, NY: Orchard Books, 1988.

Sometimes I Think I Hear My Name. New York, NY: Pantheon, 1982.

Sophia's War. New York, NY: Beach Lane Books, 2012.

S.O.R. Losers. New York, NY: Bradbury, 1984.

Strange Happenings: Five Tales of Transformation. New York, NY: Harcourt, 2006.

Things That Sometimes Happen: Thirty Very Short Stories for Very Young People. New York, NY: Atheneum Books for Young Readers, 2002.

Tom, Babette & Simon: Three Tales of Transformation. New York, NY: Macmillan Books for Young Readers, 1995.

The Traitor's Gate. New York, NY: Atheneum/Richard Jackson Books, 2007.

The True Confessions of Charlotte Doyle. New York, NY: Orchard Books, 1990.

What Do Fish Have to Do with Anything? Cambridge, MA: Candlewick, 2004.

Who Stole the Wizard of Oz? New York, NY: Knopf, 1981.

Who Was That Masked Man, Anyway? New York, NY: Orchard Books, 1992.

Windcatcher. New York, NY: Bradbury, 1991.

Wolf Rider. New York, NY: Bradbury, 1986.

The Book Without Words: A Fable of Medieval Magic

"[*The Book Without Words*] will surely keep readers turning pages. Odo's cleverness and cynicism make him a likable character, while Sybil's innate goodness will endear her to readers. Clearly this is a story with a message, a true fable. Thoughtful readers will devour its absorbing plot and humorous elements, and learn a useful truth along the way." —*School Library Journal*

Catch You Later, Traitor

"Avi, a master of historical fiction, vividly recreates not only the neighborhoods and pop culture of period Brooklyn, but the runaway paranoia that dominated daily life in the early years of the Cold War…this novel succeeds on every level." —*School Library Journal*

"Avi's tale of one Brooklyn family living in a time of intolerance effectively explores the natures of suspicion, loyalty, and freedom, following a young protagonist who comes to learn the importance of freedom of speech." —*Horn Book Magazine*

Poppy and Ereth

"This heartwarming fantasy is filled with fast-moving action and danger, and has themes of friendship and loss. Fans of the series will be completely satisfied." —*School Library Journal*

Sophia's War: A Tale of the Revolution

"Newbery Medalist Avi (*Crispin: The Cross of Lead*) channels the mood, language, and danger of the Revolutionary War in this seamless blend of history and fiction, set in British-occupied New York City. . . . Avi doesn't sugarcoat the brutal realities of war as Sophia races to find help intercepting John André, who was also a boarder in her home years earlier and her first crush, in this rich, nail-biting thriller."
— *Publishers Weekly*

City of Orphans

"Heroic deeds, narrow escapes, dastardly villains, amazing coincidences and a family rich in love and hope are all part of an intricate and endlessly entertaining adventure. Terrific!" —*Kirkus Reviews*

TIMELINE

1937 Avi Wortis is born on December 23, in New York City.

1938 Avi's family moves to Brooklyn.

1942 Avi begins elementary school at PS 8.

1951 Avi flunks out during his first semester at Stuyvesant High School and transfers to Elizabeth Irwin High School.

1955 Avi writes in his journal, "I'm going to become a playwright." He graduates from high school and enters Antioch College in Ohio.

1956 Avi transfers to the University of Wisconsin in Madison and begins a double major in history and playwriting.

1959 Avi graduates from the University of Wisconsin but remains another year to do graduate work in playwriting.

1960 Avi wins the University of Wisconsin's playwriting competition. His play is produced and published in two magazines. He moves to San Francisco and gets a job as a resident playwright for the World Theater.

1961 Frustrated with the theater scene in San Francisco, Avi moves to New York City.

1962 Avi begins working as a clerk in the theater collection of the New York Public Library.

1963 Avi marries a dancer named Joan Gainer.

1964 Avi receives a master's degree in library science from Columbia University.

1966 Avi and Joan's first son, Shaun, is born.

1968 Avi and his family spend a year in England, where Avi's second son, Kevin, is born.

1970 Back in the United States, the family moves to Trenton, New Jersey, where Avi takes a job as a librarian at Trenton State College. Avi's first book for children, *Things That Sometimes Happen: Thirty Very Short Stories for Very Young People*, a short story collection, is published.

1975 Avi's first novel for young people, *No More Magic*, is published.

1976 Avi and his family move to New Hope, Pennsylvania.

1982 Avi and Joan are divorced.

1983 Avi marries Coppelia Kahn, a literature professor, and moves to Providence, Rhode Island.

1986 Avi quits working to focus entirely on writing.

1991 *The True Confessions of Charlotte Doyle* is named a Newbery Honor Book.

1992 *Nothing but the Truth* is named a Newbery Honor Book.

1995 After separating from Kahn, Avi moves to Colorado—first to Boulder, then to Denver, where he now lives with his third wife, Linda Wright.

2003 *Crispin: The Cross of Lead* is awarded the Newbery Medal.

2005 Avi wins the Anne V. Zarrow Award for Young Readers' Literature.

2009 Avi is awarded the Beacon of Freedom Award for *Iron Thunder*.

2014 Avi wins the Notable Wisconsin/Illustrator Award for 2014.

GLOSSARY

APPENDICES A portion of extra material that is located at the end of a book or document.

AUTHORITARIAN Imposing complete and rigid obedience to authority.

BLACKOUT When all lights are turned off or hidden, making it difficult for enemy aircraft to drop bombs on targets.

BOTANIST A scientist who specializes in the study of plants.

BROWNSTONE A house built with reddish-brown stones.

CLIFFHANGER An ending to a story that leaves the audience in anticipation of what will happen next.

COMMUNISM A political theory based on the ideas of Karl Marx, in which a society's property is owned by the public.

CONVENTIONS Standard rules of conduct or behavior.

DYSGRAPHIA A writing disability that leads to misspelling of words and inversion of letters.

DYSLEXIA A disorder that includes trouble learning to read or understand words, letters, or other symbols.

EPIC An artwork, such as a novel or poem, of grand, heroic size and subject matter.

EXPLOITATIVE Using someone else for selfish reasons.

INDENTURED SERVANT A servant who is bound to a master by contract.

MALAMUTE A breed of Alaskan dog used to pull sleds.

MONARCHY A system of government in which one person, usually a king or queen, rules the country.

NEWSREEL A short film of recent news clips.

PLAYWRIGHT Someone who writes plays.

PRESTIGIOUS Distinguished, highly regarded.

QUAKER A member of a sect of Christianity known as the Religious Society of Friends that formed in seventeenth-century England. Many of its members settled in the colonies in New England.

RATION To cut down or limit one's use of a product that is scarce.

RECOIL To shrink or spring back in fear or disgust.

TOKEN An action, motion, or item that serves as a symbol.

TRAUMATIZED Psychologically hurt or damaged.

UNDERMINE To sabotage or weaken.

VICTORIAN Relating to the reign of England's Queen Victoria (1837–1901).

Association for Library Service to Children (ALSC)
50 E. Huron Street
Chicago, IL 60611
(800) 545-2433, ext. 2163
E-mail: alsc@ala.org
Website: http://www.ala.org/alsc
This organization is dedicated to supporting all library services to children.

Avi
PO Box 900
Clark, CO 80428
Website: http://www.avi-writer.com
If you'd like to write a letter to Avi directly, this is the best address. Replies, if any, can take weeks, so be patient. It helps to include a self-addressed stamped envelope.

Avi Creative Licensing
Gail Hochman
Brandt & Hochman, NYC
1501 Broadway
New York, NY 10036
Website: http://www.avi-writer.com
If you'd like Avi to come to your school to do a presentation, this is the best way to put in a request, as this is his agent.

International Literacy Association
PO Box 8139
Newark, DE 19714-8139

(800) 336-7323
E-mail: customerservice@reading.org
Website: http://www.reading.org
The International Literacy Organization is a global advocacy organization for teachers' and students' needs and the spreading of literacy.

KidsBookshelf
PO Box 3922
Olathe, KS 66063
Website: http://www.kidsbookshelf.com
Learn more about books, authors, and how to publish your writing from this website. If you'd like to write to some of your favorite authors, this website also gives you the addresses of their publishers and where to send the letter.

Reading Rockets
WETA Public Television
2775 S. Quincy Street
Arlington, VA 22206
E-mail: readingrockets@weta.org
Website: http://www.readingrockets.org
This organization focuses on helping young readers and features games, videos, and much more for readers.

Young Adult Library Services Association (YALSA)
50 E. Huron Street
Chicago, IL 60611
(800) 545-2433, ext. 4390

E-mail: YALSA@ala.org
Website: http://www.ala.org/yalsa
This is the website to go to in order to find the latest in young adult books, including awards and conferences—and just great books to check out.

WEBSITES

Because of the changing nature of Internet links, Rosen Publishing has developed an online list of websites related to the subject of this book. This site is updated regularly. Please use this link to access the list:

http://www.rosenlinks.com/AAA/Avi

FOR FURTHER READING

Bloom, Susan P., and Cathryn M. Mercier. *Presenting Avi.* New York, NY: Twayne Publishers, 1997.

Curtiss, Lucie. *Dyslexic and Un-Stoppable: How Dyslexia Helps Us Create the Life of Our Dreams and How You Can Do It Too.* Garden City, NY: Morgan James Publishing, 2014.

Dunn, Jessica. *A Teen's Guide to Getting Published: Publishing for Profit, Recognition and Academic Success.* Austin, TX: Prufrock Press, 2006.

Hambleton, Vicki, and Cathleen Greenwood. *So, You Want to Be a Writer? How to Write, Get Published, and Maybe Even Make It Big!* New York, NY: Aladdin/Beyond Words, 2012.

Hanley, Victoria. *Seize the Story: A Handbook for Teens Who Like to Write.* Austin, TX: Prufrock Press, 2008.

Johnson, Kathy. *The Roadmap from Disabilities to Success.* Burnt Hills, NY: ZLS Publishing, 2010.

Levine, Gail Carson. *Writing Magic: Creating Stories that Fly.* New York, NY: HarperCollins, 2006.

Lord, Bettie Bao. *In the Year of the Boar and Jackie Robinson.* New York, NY: HarperCollins, 2003.

Majors, Kerri. *This Is Not a Writing Manual: Notes for the Young Writer in the Real World.* Cincinnati, OH: Writer's Digest Books, 2013.

Markham, Lois. *Avi.* Santa Barbara, CA: Learning Works, 1996.

Mazer, Anne, and Ellen Potter. *Spilling Ink: A Young Writer's Handbook.* New York, NY: Square Fish, 2012.

Oelschalager, Vanita. *Knees: The Mixed Up World of*

a Boy with Dyslexia. Akron, OH: VanitaBooks LLC, 2015.

Price, Janet, and Jennifer E. Fisher. *Take Control of Dyslexia and Other Reading Difficulties.* Austin, TX: Prufrock Press, 2011.

Richards, Regina. *Eli, the Boy Who Hated to Write.* Riverside, CA: RET Center Press, 2008.

Rose, Lisa Otter. *You've Got Verve, Jamie Ireland!* North Charleston, SC: Amazon Digital Services, 2014.

Schwartz, Tina. *Writing and Publishing: The Ultimate Teen Guide.* Lanham, MD: Scarecrow Press, 2010.

Silverstein, Alvin, Virginia Silverstein and Laura Silverstein. *Handy Health Guide to Dyslexia.* Berkeley Heights, NJ: Enslow Publishers, 2014.

Speaker-Yuan, Margaret. *Avi.* Philadelphia, PA: Chelsea House Publishing, 2005.

Sutherland, Jane. *Dysgraphia: Causes, Connections and Cures.* CreateSpace, 2014.

Tait, Leia. *Avi.* Paradise CA: Paw Prints, 2011.

Warren, Tracy. *Porkie Pies and Big Fat Sausages.* Moira Brown, 2013. Kindle ed.

Wheeler, Jill. *Avi* (Children's Authors). Edina, MN: ABDO Publishing Company, 2011.

Winton, Alais. *The Self-Help Guide for Teens with Dyslexia: Useful Stuff You May Not Learn at School.* London, England: Jessica Kingsley Publishers, 2015.

BIBLIOGRAPHY

Avi. "About Avi's Books." Avi-Writer.com. Retrieved February 2003 (http://www.avi-writer.com/about-books/book_descriptions/dont_you_know_war.html). Reprinted by permission of Brandt & Hochman Literary Agents.

Avi. Acceptance speech for the Boston Globe/Horn Book Fiction Award for *The True Confessions of Charlotte Doyle. Horn Book Magazine,* January/February 1992, pp. 24–27.

Avi. "All That Glitters." *Horn Book Magazine,* September/October 1987, pp. 569–576. Reprinted by permission of Brandt & Hochman Literary Agents, Inc.

Avi. "The Barn." Avi-Writer.com. 2015. Retrieved June 8, 2015 (http://www.avi-writer.com/books/books/barn.html).

Avi. *Blue Heron.* New York, NY: Bradbury, 1992.

Avi. *Bright Shadow.* New York, NY: Bradbury, 1985.

Avi. "The Child in Children's Literature." *Horn Book Magazine,* January/February 1993, pp. 40–50.

Avi. *City of Light, City of Dark: A Comic Book Novel.* New York, NY: Orchard Books, 1993.

Avi. *Crispin: The Cross of Lead.* New York, NY: Hyperion, 2002.

Avi. *Devil's Race.* New York, NY: HarperTrophy, 1984.

Avi. *Don't You Know There's a War On?* New York, NY: HarperCollins, 2001.

Avi. *Encounter at Easton.* New York, NY: Morrow Junior Books, 1994.

Avi. "Future Classics." *Horn Book Magazine,* November/December 2000, p. 647.

Avi. "I Can Read, I Can Read!" *Horn Book Magazine,* March/April 1994, pp. 166–169. Reprinted by permission of Brandt & Hochman Literary Agents, Inc.

Avi. *The Man Who Was Poe.* New York, NY: Avon Flare, 1991.

Avi. "The Mayor of Central Park." Avi-Writer.com. 2015. Retrieved June 8, 2015 (http://www.avi-writer.com/books/books/mayor.html).

Avi. *Night Journeys.* New York, NY: Morrow Junior Books, 1994.

Avi. *Nothing but the Truth.* New York, NY: Avon Flare, 1993.

Avi: The Official Web Site. Retrieved April 2015 (http://www.avi-writer.com).

Avi. "A Place Called Ugly." Avi-Writer.com. Retrieved February 2003 (http://www.avi-writer.com/aboutbooks/book_descriptions/place_called_ugly.html). Reprinted by permission or Brandt & Hochman Literary Agents.

Avi. "Reviewing the Reviewers." *School Library Journal,* March 1986, pp. 114–115.

Avi. *Romeo and Juliet—Together (And Alive!) at Last.* New York, NY: Avon Camelot, 1988.

Avi. *The Secret School.* New York, NY: Harcourt, 2001.

Avi. "Six Secrets to Good Writing." Avi-Writer.com. 2015. Retrieved June 8, 2015 (http://www.avi-writer.com/writing/writing.html).

Avi. *Sometimes I Think I Hear My Name.* New York, NY: Avon Flare, 1995.

Avi. *S.O.R. Losers.* New York, NY: Simon & Schuster, 1984.

Avi. "The True Confessions of Charlotte Doyle." *Horn Book Magazine,* January/February 1992, p. 25–27. Reprinted by permission of Brandt & Hochman Literary Agents, Inc.

Avi. *The True Confessions of Charlotte Doyle.* New York, NY: Orchard Books, 1990.

Avi. *"Who Was That Masked Man, Anyway?"* New York, NY: Orchard Books, 1992.

Avi. *Wolf Rider.* New York, NY: Aladdin, 1993.

Avi. *Wordcraft* blog. Retrieved April 14, 2015. (http://www.avi-writer.com/blog/).

Avi and Betty Miles. "School Visits: The Author's Viewpoint." *School Library Journal,* January 1987, pp. 21–26.

Benson, Sonia. *Something About the Author.* Vol. 71. Diane Teligen, ed. Detroit: Gale Group, 1993.

Bloom, Susan R, and Cathryn M. Mercier. *Presenting Avi.* New York, NY: Twayne Publishers, 1997.

Burns, Mary M. "Review of *S.O.R. Losers.*" *Horn Book Magazine.* January 1985, p. 49.

Educational Paperback Association. "Author Biographies: Avi." January 2003. Retrieved April 2015 (http://www.edupaperback.org/author-bios/avi.html).

Folk, Jennifer. "Avi Wortis." Pennsylvania State University. July 2007. Retrieved April 12–13, 2015. (http://pabook.libraries.psu.edu/palitmap/

bios/Wortis__Avi.html).

Horn Book Magazine. "Review of *Beyond the Western Sea*." *Horn Book Magazine,* July/August 1996, p. 461.

Jackson, Richard. "We." *Horn Book Magazine,* May/June 1993, pp. 296–302.

Jaffee, Cyrisse. "Review of *Emily Upham's Revenge*." *School Library Journal,* March 1978, p. 124.

Jones, Trev. "Review of *The True Confessions of Charlotte Doyle*." *School Library Journal,* September 1990, p. 221.

KidSpace@the Internet Public Library. "The Author Page: Avi." Retrieved April 2015 (http://www.ipl.org/div/kidspace/askauthor/Avi.html).

KidsReads.com. "Avi Interview." Retrieved April 2015 (http://www.kidsreads.com/authors/au-avi. asp).

Marinak, Barbara Ann. "Interview with Avi." *Book Report,* March/April 1992, p. 26.

Markham Lois. *Avi.* Santa Barbara, CA: The Learning Works, 1996.

Mercier, Catherine M. "Review of *The True Confessions of Charlotte Doyle*." *The Five Owls,* January/February 1991, p. 57.

New York Public Library. "Author Chat with Avi." Live Chat July 30, 2003. Retrieved April 13–14, 2015 (http://www.nypl.org/author-chat-avi).

O'Connor, Jane. "Review of *Captain Grey*." *New York Times Book Review,* September 11, 1977, p. 30.

Scholastic Books. "About the Author. Avi's Biography." Retrieved April 2015 (http://www2.scholastic .com/teachers/authorsandbooks).

Scholastic Books. Transcript of interview with Avi. Retrieved April 2015 (http ://www2.scholastic.com/teachers/authorsandbooks).

Senick, Gerald J., ed. *Children's Literature Review.* Vol. 24. Detroit, MI: Gale Group, 1991.

SimonSaysKids.com. "Authors and Illustrators: Avi." Retrieved April 2015 (http://www.simonsays.com/subs/pdfs/kids/Avi.pdf).

Stan, Susan. "Conversations: Avi." *The Five Owls,* January/February 1990, p. 45.

Sutherland, Zena. "Review of *The Fighting Ground.*" Bulletin of the Center for Children's Books, June 1984, p. 180.

Sutton, Roger. "Review of *The Man Who Was Poe.*" Bulletin of the Center for Children's Books, October 1989, p. 27.

INDEX

ABOUT THE AUTHORS

Tamra Orr is a full-time author living in the Pacific Northwest with her husband, children, dog, and cat. She spends her time researching and writing and has written more than four hundred books for all ages. She is a graduate of Ball State University and loves reading and writing books of all kinds. Learning about authors helps her discover new ways of looking at the world and using words to describe it.

Michael A. Sommers was born in Texas and raised in Canada. After earning a bachelor's degree in English literature at McGill University in Montreal, Canada, he completed a master's degree in history and civilizations from the École des Hautes Études en Sciences Sociales in Paris, France. He has worked as a writer and photographer.

PHOTO CREDITS

Cover, p. 3 Katherine Warde; pp. 6-7, 30-31, 60 © AP Images; pp. 12-13 Ed Clark/The LIFE Picture Collection/Getty Images; p. 15 Adam Dance/Moment Mobile/Getty Images; p. 23 Bernard Hoffman/The LIFE Picture Collection/Getty Images; p. 33 Rae Russel/Archive Photos/Getty Images; p. 36 New York Daily News/Getty Images; p. 41 Universal Images Group/Getty Images; p. 45 CristinaMuraca/Shutterstock.com; p. 48 John Greim/LightRocket/Getty Images; p. 62 De Agostini Picture Library/Getty Images; pp. 66-67 DEA/A. De Gregorio/De Agostini/Getty Images; p. 75 kurdistan/Shutterstock.com; pp. 78-79 George Rose/Getty Images; p. 85 Portland Press Herald/Getty Images; cover, interior pages (book) © www.istockphoto.com/Andrzej Tokarski, (textured background) javarman/Shutterstock.com; interior pages (sun and water) Valentin Valkov/Shutterstock.com

Designer: Nicole Russo; Editor: Heather Moore Niver; Photo Researcher: Heather Moore Niver